THE LIFE OF

A CHIMNEY BOY

THE CHIMNEY BOY IN AFTER YEARS.

THE LIFE OF
A CHIMNEY BOY

WRITTEN BY HIMSELF

EDITED AND CONCLUDED BY

Rev. J. ARTHUR TURNER

" Jesus—My Saviour !"

London:

CHARLES H. KELLY

2, CASTLE ST., CITY RD.; AND 26, PATERNOSTER ROW, E.C.

1901

PREFACE

T HE best introduction that we can give to this little book is a quotation from Robert Mackenzie's intensely interesting *History of the Nineteenth Century*.

Referring to the time of our hero's boyhood, he writes:— "People used to employ not only little boys but sometimes little girls of five and six to sweep their chimneys. Some of the chimneys were very awkwardly built in those days, and the child was compelled to crawl into them, often driven by blows to the horrid work.

"Sometimes the chimney was not sufficiently cooled, and the child was burnt. Often he stuck fast in a narrow flue, and was extricated with difficulty. Occasionally he was taken out dead. Parliament refused for some time to suppress these atrocities, even after a machine could be got for fifteen shillings which swept chimneys better than the climbing boy did.

"The barbarous custom of making boys climb was unknown excepting in England, where it originated about the beginning of the eighteenth century. By the time the boy was sixteen he was ordinarily too big for the occupation, and found himself helpless, without a trade, and very frequently with enfeebled health. This method of cleaning chimneys by climbing boys was not suppressed till 1840."

That these pages may serve to make

the young people who read them thankful for their own happier lot, — sympathetic towards our suffering brothers and sisters whose life is a desperate struggle for bread,—and lead them to love and trust in the same Saviour who sustained this poor chimney boy through all his cruel lot—is our prayer.

CONTENTS

ILLUSTRATIONS

THE LIFE OF

A CHIMNEY BOY

———◆———

CHAPTER I

A CHILD'S CRUEL LOT

SEVERAL of my friends having wished me to write the story of my life, I will try and do so as far as I can, trusting it may be for the glory of God, and for the benefit of any young people who may be left in the world friendless, as I was.

My father was a sweep, and my three brothers also followed the same trade. Our home was at Stepney, in East London, until ill-health compelled my father to give up his business, when he sold the goodwill, and left me with the man who bought it, to learn the trade. I was only about six years old at the time, and really too young for the work, so they made me do little odd things about the house, such as lighting the fires and nursing the baby. This arrangement lasted for about six months, when one of the lads took me with him to teach me how to climb my first chimney. He carried me up with my feet planted on his shoulders, and showed me how the climbing was done; but that was all, for he left me there at the top, to return the best way I could. You will not be surprised to hear that I fell down upon the fire-grate, and the wonder is that I was not killed at the start.[1]

It is a great deal harder to learn to come down a chimney than to go up. The work gave me very sore knees and elbows, so that for nearly six months I had to have them bathed with salt and water every day.

I am sorry to say that my mistress was a confirmed drunkard, and pawned everything she could lay hands on for gin. But fortunately I did not have to remain in her miserable house very long; and sad to say, soon after I left, she ended her life and that of her baby in the river.

My second place was with a sweep at Poplar, who was also a drunkard, and accustomed to stay away from home for three and four days together. As he had no wife to provide things for us, my

[1] See Preface.

brother and I often got but little food to eat.

My father, on hearing of our sad case, came down one day while my master was out, and took us both away to a situation in the West End, near Hyde Park. This was in 1840. Here the work was very hard. We often had to get up at half-past two in the morning, and climb the chimney soon after three o'clock.

One morning, two of us went to Hyde Park Gardens. On entering the kitchen chimney, we found that it had a very long slope in it, and the soot from the upright part, as it fell, blocked the slope, so that it was difficult to get air to breathe, and it took one boy all his time to keep a clear opening, and so save us both from suffocation.

On one occasion the soot was on fire in a similar slope, but I did not know it till I had climbed part of the way up the upright, when the smoke almost suffocated me. I hurried to the top as fast as I could, but found to my dismay a long chimney - pot there. It was evident I could not get out that way, and the smoke was rising faster and faster. I saw that to stay where I was would be certain death, so down I went. In about a minute my feet were in the burning soot; but I struggled through, and escaped, not much the worse for my adventure. My mates threw water over me, to extinguish the smouldering soot still clinging to my shirt. The only other garment which we wore when climbing was a pair of leather knee-breeches. I was twelve years of age when the Lord thus saved my life.

We sweep boys only washed once a week, then we were allowed to sleep over in the house. Saturday night and Sunday we were quite gentlemen, dressed out in blue suits of clothes and high hats. But when Monday morning came, all that was changed. We had to run over to the soot warehouse in our shirts and get our work-day clothes on. The distance was about two hundred yards. Here we four boys slept all the week, in a place very much like a cupboard, where the dust was almost choking.

One of the older sweeps with whom we worked was of a very covetous disposition, which he showed by taking away from us all the nice pieces of tart that tender-hearted cooks gave us, and some of the pence which kind ladies bestowed on us as well.

Part of our work was to go and get the mortar out of the bends of new chimneys, and to remove the rubbish which the labourers threw down inside, instead of carrying it down the ladder. We have sometimes removed as much as a cartload out of the chimneys of a large house.

One day three of us boys got blocked in a chimney that had several slopes in it, and being unable to move either way, the journeyman had to cut a hole in the brick-work to let us out. Often also the lime made our tongues bleed. On one occasion the men were cruel enough to put me in at the top of a chimney on fire, when I was obliged to go right through it to the bottom, sweeping it with my body as I went.

We brothers continued at this dreadful work till 1842, when the new Act came into force which did away with chimney boys. But for years after this date, boys still climbed in country places.

With the incoming of better days, my father had a sweeping machine given him by a kind friend.   He then took us to live with him at Coleshill, near Amersham, where he remained for some time.   After about nine months, my youngest brother and I moved to Wooding.   My father's health then failing, we all went back again to London.

CHAPTER II

THE PERILS OF A CHIMNEY BOY

IN August 1843 my father died. It was like losing father and mother together, for I am sorry to say my mother was a very helpless woman. A few months later I got a letter written to my uncle at Coleshill, asking if he knew of a place suitable for me. He replied that he had found me one at Mill End, near Rickmansworth. So I was taken in a cart as far as Amersham, and from there I found my way to my uncle's house.

But as I was going along the road where

my father had led me not long before, I felt so broken-hearted that I sat down and wept, and, in my extremity of grief, asked *God* to be my Father and Guide. It often fills my heart with gratitude when I remember how God has answered that prayer. Faithfully He has kept me up to the present time, and I know He will be with me to the end of my journey.

I soon found that my new place was far from being a smooth one, and when they began to lay the rope about my back I started to run away; but not knowing which way to go to better my lot, strange and friendless as I was in that part of the country, I had no choice but to endure it.

The first year I only had my clothes and food found. Later on my mistress generously paid me the sum of *one pound a year* as wages; but lest I should be lifted up beyond measure, she laid the fire-irons about my head if I did not clean them to her liking. In this treatment, however, I was not alone, for she served her own children in the same way. Her husband, my employer, was "Jack of all trades," being sweep, carpenter, and publican in one.

I had quite a little adventure one day at Lord Ebury's mansion, Moor Park. Ascending the stillroom chimney, I found a long narrow slope in it, which rapidly became filled with the soot I swept down from above, so that I was nearly suffocated in attempting to get back. Finding it impossible to return the same way, I went up to the top again, and, climbing out on to the roof, tried to get in at one of the trap-doors, but without success. So I descended the chimney a second time, rapping with my brush all the way. This roused Lord Ebury, who went downstairs and gave the alarm. In the meantime, however, I had found an iron slide in the chimney. This I opened, and came through into the drawing-room! There I walked from one door to another, trying to find the best way out ; the soot meanwhile, running down my breeches, littered the white damask floor-covering.

Just at this point in came Lord Ebury, with the butler and my master, crying out, "What is the matter?" and "Was I hurt?" On receiving the answer "No," he then inquired why my master did not sweep the chimneys with a machine. When he explained to him that it would be impossible without a great deal of alteration in the chimneys, he gave orders at once that the bricklayer should carry out the necessary improvements. Thus

my peril was overruled of God for the
good of others.

At Lord Essex' mansion, Watford, I
once had a narrow escape, for as I was
going up one of the chimneys the side fell
out, carrying me with it on to the tower.
Had it been the other side instead, I must
certainly have been killed; but this time
also God spared my life, because He had
a work for me to do.

Another day, when we were there, we
had to wait till eleven o'clock to sweep
a bedroom chimney, because the Queen
Dowager was staying there at the time,
and was not yet up. She was very
much interested in my work, and took
the opportunity of asking me if I liked
chimney climbing. I told her " No."
She then asked several other questions,
and ordered one of her maids to give me
a cup of tea with bread-and-butter, while

the Queen herself was condescending enough to give me half a crown. I look back with pleasure on this incident, and may here add that I read only a short time ago of her happy death, and this showed me how the love of Christ can smooth the pillow of the rich as well as of the poor. *His* riches are the true riches, such as the world cannot give.

There was a good school at Mill End which many of the boys from Rickmansworth attended, and I being a sweep, was considered good sport for them, especially when there was snow on the ground. Now, every evening I had to go nearly into the town for milk. One wintry day, when the earth was covered with its white carpet, I took the precaution before I started to fill my pockets with soot. As soon as I left the village, I noticed that these boys had got a heap of snowballs

MOOR PARK, RICKMANSWORTH.

ready for me. So I went up to them and
said—

"What are you going to do with these?"

"Snowball you," they replied.

"Are you?" said I, and with that I
threw a handful of soot into their faces
quickly, one after the other. You should
have seen them make off at full gallop, I
after them! From that time they took
good care to keep out of my way.

Near Mill End there was a house which
was nearly always empty. People said it
was haunted, and that about twelve o'clock
at night you might see the ghosts dancing
up and down inside the window - panes.
Thinking I should rather like to see a
ghost, I went one night and took my
stand in the meadow opposite to watch;
but though I stayed a good long time,
I am bound to say *I saw nothing*.

At this time I always went to the

Sunday school whenever I could, and to the Sunday evening service as well. I have always loved the Sunday school, for it was there that I met the kind friend who took me to his night school and taught me to write. But I was often kept away by Sunday work, as it was the time when Feargus O'Connor was building the thirty - five houses for his colony of Chartist weavers at Herons-gate.[1] My master used to fetch and take him to and from Watford Station, and I remained at home to look after the horse and trap.

I also had to clean out the flues of the paper mill on the Lord's Day. At such times, the boys of the village, knowing how I wished to be at the school instead, jeered at me as I passed in my sooty clothes, and said—

[1] See Note A, p 87.

" There goes the meetinger."

But I knew I was right in the sight
of God, for I felt even at that early
age His Holy Spirit striving within me,
and often when I saw the young people
baptized, wished I was amongst them.

I had a very kind and loving Sunday-
school teacher named Wright, who afterwards lived at Sarratt. It was there also
that he died very suddenly while attend-
ing a prayer-meeting. I cut out the
account of his death and glued it into
my Family Bible, telling my children to
let it always remain there.

On week-nights I played with the other
boys of the village, but had no company
with them on Sundays. Unlike myself,
they seemed bent on evil, and I have since
found out that in after life several of them
were transported out of the country. One
of the companions of my boyhood met

me a few years ago, and said he had been nearly all over the world. He did not seem to me much changed, although he professed to be a better man and a tee-totaller, so I told him that total abstinence alone would not take him to heaven. I often thank God that He has always kept me from using bad language, and from love of the ale-house, which has been the ruin of thousands.

After about four years at Mill End, I began to grow too big for some of the smaller chimneys, and I had to climb them naked. That is what we called "buffin' at them." One morning, my master (evidently feeling that I was slipping out of his hands), before he went to his carpentry work, called me to him and asked if I had been looking out for another place. On my replying that I had, he raised his hand and gave me such a violent box on the ears that he felled me to the ground.

I began now to think that it was indeed time for me to leave, for it was evident they were getting tired of me, and I never knew what they might do next. So I went to another sweep at Rickmansworth, who took me on at half a crown a week, with my food. I had to help him in the bricklaying trade as well.

At this wage I felt I was quite a gentleman, and let most of my money run on, till it amounted to thirty-five shillings, when I bought a watch. Then I let it mount up again, till they owed me about four pounds. After this, I drew the money and went to London to see my brothers and my uncle, leaving three pounds in my uncle's care.

When I came back, my master wanted to know what I had done with the money. I told him. He then said he did not give me the money to save, but to buy new clothes with. This was on Monday. When Saturday came, and dinner was over, he said—

"We shall not want you any more, so you can go, for we know you are preparing to leave us in the lurch."

In vain I replied that I had no thought of any such thing. They would not believe me. They refused also to pay me the balance of my wages, which amounted to ten shillings, so I had to pack up and start off just as I was, without any money to help me on the way. But God had prepared me unexpected friends.

I took off my boots, and tying them to my bundle, slung them over my shoulder and started for London. It was a wet day. When I got to Pinner, there was a coal waggon going in the same direction.

I asked the men to give me a ride, which they willingly did. They inquired where I was going. In reply I told them all about my affairs, for to my joy I found they were Christian men and teetotallers. Stopping at Harrow, they baited their horses, and gave me some coffee and bread - and - cheese. The journey was slow, but at last we got to London, and before we parted they expressed the wish that we might all meet in heaven. I clearly saw God's goodness in this affair also, and went on my way wondering if we should know each other again in heaven.

I had almost forgotten to mention several other accidents which befell me while at Mill End. One morning about four o'clock, as we were going to Chalfont to work, my young master drove over me in the darkness.

At another time I was riding on the top

of a load of grass, when we passed through a shallow stream, and the jolting of the stones dislodged part of the load, bringing me down with it into the water; but I escaped with no greater discomfort than being obliged to remain in my wet clothes all day.

I had a narrow escape also in passing through the heating - pipes of Rickmansworth parish church, which ran from one end of the building to the other. While I was inside, the bricklayer opened a trap-door at the farther end of the flue, and the draught of air blew a cloud of soot along, completely covering my head. I was nearly suffocated before I could scramble out.

The paper mill chimneys were the most dangerous to us sweep boys, and both at Loudwater and Common Moor[1] I had

[1] Note B, p. 88.

RICKMANSWORTH WESLEYAN CHURCH.

two or three very narrow escapes. The latter mill I greatly disliked, for not only did I have to give up every other Sunday to working there, but some of the flues were very hot, and under the boiler the soot was soaked into a black, muddy paste.

Putting all things together, I do not wonder that I now suffer with pains in all my limbs and in my head. But my God will give me grace to *suffer*, as He has given me grace to *do* His will in the past. I wish not to murmur; but rather, as I look back upon these many deliverances and see how God has rescued me out of so many dangers, I feel I ought to praise Him,—and I will, as long as He lends me breath.

I am sorry to have to add that while I lived at Rickmansworth I was once guilty of breaking the law. It was like this. I joined a young man who was going down to a certain place on Common Moor to catch young rabbits; but we had not been there long before the keeper saw us and came in pursuit. To avoid being caught and locked up, we were obliged to wade through a deep stream, run up the lane, and conceal ourselves among the tall stalks of a cornfield until he had gone past.

Truly the way of transgressors is hard, for by this means I was obliged to stay all the day on the moor to get my clothes dry, and I lost my dinner into the bargain. And not only did I suffer from hunger and wet, but I felt in my conscience that I had done wrong.

CHAPTER III

A SWEEP'S BATTLES

WHEN I went to London I bought a donkey and cart, to carry round vegetables and wood for sale, because my uncle wished me to get out of " the black trade." For some months I kept on at this new work; but not liking it, I returned to chimney sweeping at one and sixpence a week and my food, generally rising as early as four in the morning.

My youngest brother now came and joined me, working for his food and clothes only. After I had been in my new place a little while, I thought I would begin to save all I could, so I got a stone jar and fastened a bung in it, with a hole cut through, big enough to put money in. I took up some of the bricks under the bed in the cellar where we slept, and placed the jar in the ground, covering the spot carefully with the bricks again, but in such a way that I could drop the coins between them into the jar. When I left I think I had saved nearly five pounds.

One day we had a disagreement with our master. My brother and I had gone to a brewery to clean out the boiler flues, which we found very hot and very small. My brother came to me in one of the flues and told me that the part he was expected to sweep was so hot that he could not enter it. I told him he must refuse to go in. Hereupon our master was greatly upset, and angrily wanted to know if

I had been "giving my brother good advice." I said, " Yes, I have. The last words my father spoke to me were, 'Take care of Tom.' And I will see to it that he does not go in there to be burnt."

After this we could not get on together at all. I had sprained my ankle, and been to the London Hospital about it. The doctors said—

" You must rest it a month."

I told them I could not do so, as I had no home.

" Then we can do nothing for you," they replied.

To further punish me, my master made me do all the longest walking journeys. Many times I have sat down on the door-steps in the early morning and cried for pain. At last I was compelled to give notice to leave.

The next day he took my young brother

out and gave him drink, intending to get from him all the information he could about me. He wanted especially to know if I had any money saved (as he saw I had been careful), and what I was going to do next. I had warned my brother not to let out any of our secrets, for I guessed what was his purpose in this new move ; and as soon as I heard what he had been doing, I advised my brother to give notice to leave also. My master gave him his clothes that very morning, and turned him away there and then. I stayed the week out, but he refused to give me either food or work.

When my week was up, I asked for my clothes and my watch and the seven and sixpence which was due to me. He gave me my clothes and watch, but refused to pay the money, so I put it into Court.

As it would be three weeks before the

case came up and I could not stand still so long doing nothing, I bought a sweeping machine, and began to get some orders on my own account, so as to obtain food for my brother and myself. We occupied a small room in my aunt's house. The money was paid before Court day. I now made up my mind to stay at Limehouse, though I did intend at first to start in some new place. God had ordered it otherwise.

For three or four years I had great persecution to endure from my former employer, who set his men to pitch into me and fight me in the streets. One morning a sweep came upon me all at once, intending to throw me down; but I was on my guard, and quick as thought, gave him a twist over on the other side. Down he went, with his head on the pavement, and myself on top of him. After that he thought well to go quietly home, and henceforth let me alone.

At another time, when a certain lady had been waiting for this same sweep for some hours, she grew impatient, and sent for me. When I had almost done the work, he arrived, and flinging my tools into the road, told his man to put me out after them. But he was not strong enough, and it took the two of them to do it. The lady of the house meanwhile seized the poker and threatened to "split their cowardly heads open if they did not let me alone." A policeman now arriving on the scene, was informed by the lady how they had treated me, with the result that my enemy was fined forty shillings and bound over to keep the peace.

Some months after this he sent another of his men to my house, after I had been to the London Hospital to see a child of

AN EAST END SWEEP.

mine, only eighteen months old, that had been scalded nearly to death. When I came home, this man was watching for me. He waited till I got in, then knocked at the door. I opened it. Instantly he struck me through my high hat with the brush which he had brought in his hand. But seeing the blood run down over my coat, he was afraid, and made off. Again I was obliged in self-defence to take out a summons, but he contrived to disappear for a few days. On his return I got an execution against him, and this ended all my trouble in that direction.

CHAPTER IV

REMEMBERING GOD

I NOW began to be known, and business increased. I had already found a sober young woman who became my wife. We were married over forty years ago. One day, after we had been together about three years, I was in my parlour, looking round my comfortable home, when I remembered Who had helped me and given me all these things. I said to myself, "It is God. Yet I do not love Him!" But Satan whispered in my ears—

"You have been a very good young

man. You have neither been a drunkard nor a swearer."

" No," I replied aloud, "*but I am afraid to die !*" And there and then I made up my mind to go to God's house.

When Sunday came, I went in the morning to " an upper room " in Church Row, Limehouse, the place which my neighbour attended. There I heard the way of salvation explained. Full of joy at the glad tidings, I resolved to be a Christian, and immediately went home and told my wife. A young man whom I employed was sitting by at the time, and sneeringly remarked—

" Are *you* going to be religious ? "

" Yes, I am," was my instant reply.

In the evening I went again, and stayed to the prayer - meeting. There was a sister present who was praying for me, I could tell. She set my soul on fire, for she was such a praying woman as I have heard my grandmother talk about, down in Manchester. My grandmother was herself a Methodist for sixty years.

It was about two Sundays before Christmas when I began to change my thoughts. And now I was in a great fix, for I had ordered in eighteen gallons of ale for the Christmas festivities. My brother was coming to see me, also my companion and friend, with his wife and family. I knew not what to do. All that Christmas-time I was wretched. I could not play cards nor other games as I had done at former times. None of my friends could make me out, but they concluded I must be ill.

I asked the Lord to spare me till New Year's night. I then went to the prayer-meeting before the watch-night service. There I poured out my soul in prayer, found the peace which passeth understanding, and went on my way rejoicing. Ever since then I have been rejoicing. I am rejoicing in the Lord to-day while I write these words.

How many times I have sung that hymn—

Oh! happy day!
When Jesus washed my sins away.

The angel said to Mary, "Thou shalt call His name Jesus, for He shall save His people *from* their sins," not *in* them, as some will have it.

I gave up the devil's toys and pleasures, Sunday trade, dishonesty, and my former companion. By the grace of God I made a full surrender. And I have never once been sorry for it, or wished to go back to them again; but, on the other hand, I feel in my heart a perfect hatred of everything like sin. Many have told me that

I am too religious, but I feel to-day that I come far short of what I should like to be.

Anxious to tell others of the Saviour I had found, I went the Sunday following my conversion, and got a class of boys to teach. Very much of the happiness of my life I owe to my connection with the Sunday school. And ever since that day I have kept in close touch with this work. And indeed I never made it a practice to stay at home on Sunday afternoons, until these last few years, when my health and hearing have failed me. If not out in the villages preaching, I always went to the school or visited the sick.

As soon as I got saved I began to bring others to Jesus. I had three brothers who were not following Him. I went to the worst first, and would not let him rest. One night he got quite angry with me, and said he did not know how it was I was always *at him* about religion. How well I remember it! We parted at the Limehouse toll-gate. It seems but yesterday. My words were—

"Well, Joseph, I won't say anything more to you about religion for the present."

But I kept on praying for him. About two weeks after this he came down to tea, and in the evening we went to Bath Street Chapel together. There was a good work going on at the time. Several went up to the penitent form, and while I was on my knees praying for him, suddenly he pushed me aside, saying, "I can't stand it any longer." He joined the other penitents at the communion rail, and gave himself to Jesus. Oh, how happy I was then!

In after days he would often say to me,

" Brother, I can understand now why you would not let me rest in my wicked way. Religion has made me so happy within." About seven years later he died. One of the brethren went to see him before he passed away, and said—

" Brother L——, if it is well with you, wave your arm."

He gave the sign, and not long after went home to God.

Next I set about winning my youngest brother and his wife. This was a few years after. I was spending a Sunday with my friends at Limehouse, for I lived at H—— then. My brother came out in the prayer-meeting and gave himself to Christ, and again I had the greatest of earthly joys.

The minister seeing my delight, said—

" Do you know this young man ? "

" Yes," I replied ; " he is my brother."

" Ah, that is what makes you so happy, then."

I do not know when my other brother was converted, but he has been a member for some years.

I tried also to bring my old companion and friend to Christ. He did not forsake me all at once, but one Sunday he came to my house and found me reading the Bible. I did not talk with him much. This offended him, and he said—

" Put that book away. You will either have to give that up or me."

" John," I said, " I shall not give up the Bible."

At once he put on his hat and left the house, and, sad to say, that closed for ever our companionship.

Some time after, when I was on a visit to my brother, I met him yet once again, and tried hard to persuade him to come with us to God's house, but in vain. There were several other Christian sweeps present, so two or three of us prayed for him as he sat in his chair. When I got up, I took him by the hand and said—

"Do come with us."

"You can take a horse to the water," said he, "but you cannot make him drink."

"Surely you don't mean to be so obstinate as that," I replied.

"Well," he answered, "I will believe the Bible if you will explain it all to me."

I told him I should never be able to do that. So he is outside the kingdom until now.

One day I went to see a poor widow who earned her living by mangling. She was very ill at the time. But when I told her about the love of Jesus, she was led to trust Him with her soul. After that

she would often say to me, her face
lighting up with joy—

"Mr. L——, you come like an angel of
God, to tell me about Jesus."

For several months she lingered, then
as the end drew near, she gathered her
children around her (most of whom were
grown up and married), urging them to
love the Saviour, and not to live as she
herself had done.

I have often said that if persons who
call themselves the followers of Jesus
were to do a little more sick-visiting they
would become better Christians. I have
had some of my happiest times in the
sickroom, singing, reading, and praying
there with the lonely ones.

Here is one case which I call to mind.
When spending a few days with a friend
at Watford who was a Baptist, I was asked
by his wife to go and see a young woman

lying ill close by.   I went, and found her in a sad state of mind.   She said she had been deceiving herself for thirteen years. I prayed with her, and sang three or four hymns which I knew without the book, told her of the precious promises of God, and applied them to her case.

Some weeks after, I had a letter from my friend's wife saying that this young woman would like to see me once more before she died ; so I went from Limehouse to Watford on purpose, and found her rejoicing in the Lord.   She said Satan sometimes came and told her it was all a delusion.   But she then pointed him to the very spot at the foot of the bed where she sat when Jesus spoke peace to her soul and forgave her all her sins.   I went home very happy.

CHAPTER V

A NOVEL MISSIONARY IN THE KITCHEN

OH, what joy I have had in trying to bring others to Christ! I had many opportunities when I went into all classes of houses to sweep chimneys, of leaving tracts and speaking to servants.

One morning I was talking to a cook about Christ, when the lady of the house came down into the kitchen and wanted to know what was the matter.

"There is nothing the matter," I said; "only I was talking to your servant about Jesus."

"I suppose you belong to the Methodists, then?"

"Yes," I replied, "I meet with the Wesleyan people."

"Well, you had better convert *her*," she added.

I told her I could not do that, but the Holy Spirit could.

At another house the master offered me a glass of ale, "to wash the dust down." I told him I did not take ale.

"Then you are a teetotaller, I suppose?"

"Yes."

"I do not believe in that," said he. "What do you think God sent it for, if we are not to drink it?"

"God never sent it," I replied, "though He sends the things with which men make it. God made man upright, but he has 'sought out many inventions,' and I believe this is one of them."

About two years afterwards, I met the same gentleman again. He asked me if I remembered the above conversation at his house. I did not. So he reminded me of it once more, and added that he had looked up the passage referred to, and had been an abstainer ever since. He felt he was now a better man and a better Sunday-school teacher for his decision.

While I was staying in the East End of London, a farmer who used to buy my soot invited me to go down into the country and spend a few days. It was hay-making time when I went, and I worked in the fields all the day, to convince his men that they were wrong when they said a teetotaller could not do hay-making.

Presently the farmer wanted me to fetch the men's beer. But I refused, saying, "I do not drink it, and I will not fetch it." For over forty years I have not had a glass of beer or spirits in my hands, or given strong drink to any one, or paid for any to drink it. I know I have lost a lot of trade by this. But I have been willing to do so, because I know that whatever I lose here for Christ's sake and His cause will be made up to me in the world to come.

The same night, when I went to bed, this farmer overheard me at prayer, and asked if he might come in. He cried like a child while I talked to him about Jesus and His love and eternal life. He said he did not like to think of eternity. Did I?

"Yes," I replied.

"Then you are a happy man," said he.

I told him I knew that before.

He added, "There are some hard sayings in the Bible."

I asked which they were.

He then quoted, "Not many wise, not many mighty, not many noble are called," and "How hardly shall they that have riches enter into the kingdom of God."

But I said, "Your riches never need keep *you* out of heaven."

I was told not long before that he had given eight thousand pounds for a farm, though he was then over seventy years of age. He has since passed away, and I hope he found mercy of the Lord before he went.

I had a class of boys at Limehouse Sunday school, one of whom was a great trouble to me, so much so that another teacher said—

"Brother L——, I cannot think how you can do with that boy."

"Let him alone," I replied; "he will be better some day."

A few years after, when I had moved

to St. John's Wood, he came up to see me and to tell me that he was now a Sunday-school teacher himself, and secretary of the Band of Hope. He thought I should like to know this, as he had been such a trouble to me before. I have often found some of the worst boys, when converted, turn out to be the best. Having been forgiven much, they seem to love the more.

As soon as I gave my heart to God I built the family altar, and it has never since been broken down for any one. I tell all my children to remember their responsibility to God, and acknowledge Him in heart and home. They have all been lifelong abstainers. Before I was a teetotaller myself, I trained the children to habits of sobriety, but now for a long time both my wife and I have been agreed never to have any strong drink in the house. Alas! I used at one time to love it too well.

Two of my children have got safe home, one at twenty-three years of age, the other at twenty-six. I have five still living. They have all been taken to the morning Sunday school as soon as they could walk there, and *always in time*, for it has been a strong point with me to be punctual in everything, more especially in God's service. All my children are not yet on the Lord's side, but I believe they will be.

CHAPTER VI

A MESSENGER OF SATAN

AT Limehouse, in the East End of London, I was doing business with a sweep, whom I also had the joy of bringing to Jesus. He gave up the world and Sunday work at the same time. This meant a loss to him, he said, of forty pounds a year. And I can well believe it, for I myself have earned a pound in five or six hours by Sunday work, such as cleaning out boiler flues at Scott Russell's, Milwall, at the time when the *Great Eastern* was building.

I told him God would give him more than he had lost. His wife and he often used to come to my house to tea; we would then sing and pray together before we went to the services. Very happy times those were! We composed a tract between us, which we had printed, and distributed among the sweeps, to try and persuade them to give up drink, as we knew *that* was the greatest curse among them. My friend joined the Methodists at Jubilee Street, and became a teacher there.

One day, after this, just as I had started to go up to the Sunday School Union to get some books for the school, I met one of the sweeps whom we had visited. He said, "You are just the man I wanted," so I turned back with him. He then began to tell me his message, which was that he and his wife had been talking the matter over, and decided to ask me to enter into partnership with him. I told him I could not think of such a thing, as I was getting a very good living, and was also full of work at the chapel. He said "the Lord had sent him." I replied, "If the Lord has sent you, I shall be obliged to go, but I must first try and find out if it is so."

He said that one-half of his business would be more than all mine. He was in the soot trade—bought soot of the sweeps, and sold it to the farmers at a certain country market, to put on the land for manure. I asked him a few questions about how the trade was carried on, as there was a great deal of dishonesty in those days, and soot fetched a high price. I told him I should not do anything which I knew to be wrong.

To further help matters, he asked my

wife and me to come to his house to tea, that we might go over his books together. We went about two weeks after, but before beginning business I said, " Let us ask God to direct us, that we may not take a wrong step; then I shall feel safe." So we knelt down and prayed.

He said his business was worth three hundred pounds, and he wanted one hundred and fifty pounds from me if I became partner. He further added that as I was a sober young man and had a family, he would leave me in his will property which brought him in about sixty pounds a year. (Needless to say, I never received this; but as I did not expect it, I was not disappointed.)

We arranged that I was to join him in a month. Somehow I did not feel easy about it, but I prayed all the time that the Lord would guide me aright. It was agreed that we should occupy the house of one of his men, who (not long after) came down to the East End with all his belongings, and began business for himself close by us. We then packed up, and removed to St. John's Wood to fill his place.

Arriving there late at night, we lay down on the floor ; but directly we began to doze, we felt something crawling over our faces. We struck a light, and found that our bed was covered with black beetles. This was an unpleasant beginning.

About eighteen months afterwards, my partner's health failed, and the doctor told him he must retire. I then agreed to take over the whole business and pay him three hundred pounds. He moved to H——, built himself a house, and became my agent. I felt full of distrust from the first, but I came by degrees to settle it in my heart that God would not suffer me to fall. I had a Christian man at work for me, whom I took as partner, for I did not want too much business on my own shoulders, lest it should rob me of Christ.

At the end of three years I had paid the three hundred pounds with interest; but as soon as all was settled, he refused to sell any more soot for me unless I allowed him double his former commission. This he knew I could not afford. But he made my refusal an excuse to become agent for another man in the trade, and took away my customers from me. Death, however, cut short his evil deeds.

Since then I have had many hard lessons to learn. But thank the Lord, He has brought me through all my troubles, and given me the victory again and again over all my foes.

What a comfort it has been to me to know that the Lord sees my purpose has always been to live to His glory! I have kept in mind the Word of God and have taken it for my guide. Christ has been my Pattern, and the Holy Spirit my Comforter, and I have always tried to let my light shine in the world.

CHAPTER VII

LIGHT IN DARK PLACES

I HAVE had some very wicked characters to do with in my time. One day in particular I remember rebuking some men for vile conduct in a soot cellar. But the more I spoke to them the worse they behaved, till at last I threatened to report them to their master and get them turned out, or else to go away and refuse to take the soot altogether. When they saw I was determined, they gave in.

Nearly all the sweeps knew what I was, for I never wearied of preaching to them in these dark places. Sometimes one would begin to swear, then seeing me, suddenly check himself, saying, "I beg your pardon." For about thirty years I have had dealings with them, and found them as a rule a very unsteady class of men. I have just been going over in my mind one hundred and thirty-five cases of men whom I have known in the trade, and I am sorry to say that about one hundred and ten of them died drunkards.

I have seen and known some awful effects of strong drink. Several persons have asked me why I am so prejudiced against it. I tell them that if they had seen as much of the misery caused by it as I have seen, they would hate it as much as I do. Several of my friends have tried to persuade me to take a little for my asthma, but I tell them, "No; by God's help, not as long as I live, in case any one should fall through my example." That would indeed be a sad ending to the forty-one years during which I have been without strong drink, and have helped many to lead sober lives.

It has always been my wish to live to the glory of God and for the good of others. When I think of my Saviour's love to me, in saving me from sin and Satan's power these forty-two years, how can I love Him enough, or serve my neighbours enough for His sake?

Some years ago I was trying to bring a young man to Christ, when he said—

"Look at So-and-so, how he goes on."

"You must not look at those that go wrong," I replied, "but at them that go right. Now you have known me for thirteen years. Do you think I have been going right?"

"Oh yes," said he.

"Then follow me as I follow Christ." That is what Paul said, and what I have repeated to my children many times. The world takes more notice of example than of words.

One Saturday I was travelling by rail with three market gardeners. After some little general talk, one of them said—

"You belong to the Wesleyans, don't you?"

"Yes," I replied.

"Ah!" said he, "your people believe in being holy and perfect, don't they?"

"Yes, they do."

"Well, can you tell me where there is one who is holy and perfect?"

"Yes. *I am one.*"

"Oh! you are?"

"Yes," I said. "But now let me explain what I mean. I was up at four o'clock this morning, and put myself into

God's care. I have been hard at work
nearly all day, and could scarcely get here
in time to catch this train. All the time
I have been living in Christ, and Christ
has been living in me, so He makes me
holy and perfect in Himself.

"Suppose there were to be an accident
between here and H——," I went on to say;
"if this were not so, I should have to cry
out, 'Lord, wait! I am not ready!' But
when we live in God and for good, then
we are *perfect in Him* and ready for all
things."

They said that was all very well. Then
one of them asked me a foolish question
which showed clearly enough that *he* was
not living a holy life, though they all
reckoned themselves to belong to "the
elect."

CHAPTER VIII

WATCHING AND WAITING

I HAVE lived at H—— over thirty-three years, and during that time have found the greatest joy while doing my Master's work as a preacher in the villages. Often I have felt very tired when Sunday dawned, and unfit to go and preach, after getting up at three or four o'clock nearly every morning of the week before. But I have asked myself the question, "Now if I had some particular business of my own to do, should I not try and do it? How much more then when it is the *Lord's* work and

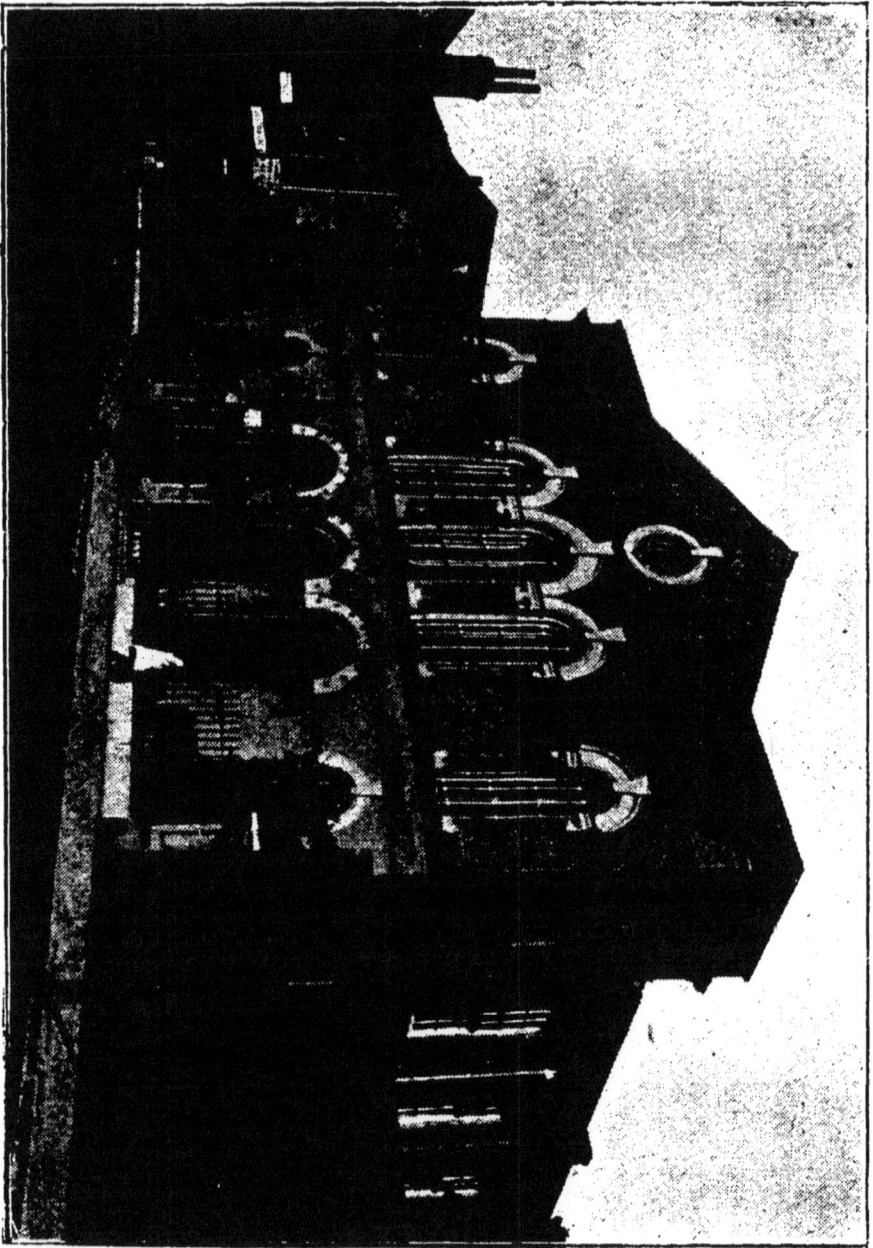

HITCHIN WESLEYAN CHAPEL.

very urgent!" I rejoice to say that I have generally come home at night feeling a better man both in body and soul.

In doing Christian work I have felt my own weakness; but at such times I have been reminded of God's word, "Not by might, nor by power, but by *My Spirit*, saith the Lord," and again, "My word shall not return unto Me void." I have proved the gospel of Christ to be "the power of God unto salvation to every one that believeth." It has been so to me, and to many whom I have known.

I have seen many dying Christians, chiefly in the villages. I have always found great delight in visiting the sick and helping them the little that I could. It has sometimes been like heaven on earth, and I have often said, "If you want to see what religion is, go and see some of God's people die. Religion is a good thing to live with, and a better thing to die with."

I always felt it a great pleasure to work for Christ. And now that I cannot do much, nor go to His house and meet with His people there, I have much of the Lord's presence with me at home. I used to say when I was younger, " I will work for Jesus Christ, who has done so much for me and for my family, while I have health, so that when I am laid by I may be able to look back and see that, as long as I could, I *did* try and win souls for Him."

In the Sunday school, while preaching indoors and out, in the sick chamber, in giving away tracts and books to the young, I know God has accepted my labours. He knows also that my eye has been single. *If I had twenty lives to live, I would give them all to Jesus, my loving Saviour, who gave Himself for me.*

During the thirty years of my life at
H—— I have always been at peace with the
brethren, and kept in mind the Saviour's
words, "Blessed are the peacemakers, for
they shall be called the children of God,"
and also how He said, "Love one another."
What a grand thing it would be if all those
who profess to love Jesus had more love
one toward another! I do not refer only
to our own people, but to all Christians.
In visiting the sick I have never made
any difference between a Methodist and a
Baptist, or any others. We are all one in
Christ, all brethren and sisters in Him.
We don't all see alike on some points,
but we must all be "washed in the blood
of the Lamb."

There are some who call themselves
Christians, but Peter calls them "busybodies about other men's matters." They
can see so much that is wrong in others,

but do not look at their own failings. As
for myself, I know that while I strive to
live every day to the Lord, yet I have
many failings. But Jesus Christ knows
I do not live in sin. Christ is my per-
fection. " I live, yet not I, but Christ
liveth in me." I know the devil does
more mischief in the church by these
"busybodies" than by people of the
world. There is too much looking at
others, and too little "looking unto Jesus."

I feel He is precious to my soul, and I
believe that all things are working together
for my good. *Though I have lost all* of this
world's goods, and my health is gone, and
the outward man is wasting away, yet
"the inward man is being renewed day
by day." When I look back and see the
way the Lord has led me all these years,
and the many friends He has sent me, I
am compelled to praise Him, and to shout

aloud for joy. *He is more precious to me than ever.*

I thank God it has been my privilege to lie down every night for many years under my Shepherd's care. How sweet is my rest! I am waiting for Him to come and fetch me home, when it is *His* time. I sometimes feel like David when he said, "Oh that I had wings like a dove, then would I fly away and be at rest." But I wish the *Lord's* will to be done, not mine.

(Here the Journal ends.)

CHAPTER IX

"JESUS—MY SAVIOUR"

OUR hero was one of those rough diamonds, at various times discovered by Methodism in unexpected places, and marvellously shaped and fitted for the Saviour's crown.

Born 11th February 1832, he was converted when about twenty-five years of age. In 1862 he moved from London to H——. Here he was indeed for many years a living epistle, known and read of all men. His pulpit efforts, though devoid of all grace of style and polish, and continually interspersed with loud "ahems,"

were so full of genuine love and Christian
experience, spiced with a touch of origin-
ality, that they went right home to the
hearts of his hearers. His face lighted up
as he spoke, while his chief theme was
ever. Jesus Christ and His full and free
salvation. When preaching at a certain
place one day, a gentleman of the con-
gregation was so delighted with his
manifest earnestness that he sent him
an unusual, but much appreciated ac-
knowledgment — the present of a brace
of partridges. Mr. L—— was a man of
prayer, and he had a wonderful power
in dealing with backsliders.

As a class leader he was a great success,
and the editor of his Journal is only one
of very many who owe much to his
paternal watchfulness and care. Scarcely
a week passed but he made an opportunity
of seeing *every* member of his large class.

If for any reason one had been absent, he would be tapped on the shoulder during the week and thus addressed, " Now, Brother So-and-so, where were you last Sunday ?　We can't have this, you know." It is only fair, however, to add that nearly all his members came to see *him*, in that crowded upper room, where the fire ran from heart to heart melting all into a blessed unity.　Oh, haste again, ye days of grace !

He went round to each member with the question, " Now, Brother So-and-so, how have you been gettin' on ? "　He would then stand immediately before the speaker, look him straight in the face, and listen intently, shading his deaf ear with his hand.

He would have no cant in the class. A member one day ventured to repeat with much unction of voice something

which he had more than once said
before, about "passing through this
waste how-l-l-ling wilderness." Losing all
patience, he broke in upon him—"Brother
So-and-so, I *won't* have it; it's *not* a
waste howling wilderness; it's a very
good world, if we only like to make
it so."

Apart from its religious ·interest as the
record from his own pen of the life of one
of Methodism's most faithful servants, the
narrative sheds a vivid light upon the
terrible life led by a poor chimney boy in
the days when chimneys were climbed,
before the great and humane Lord
Shaftesbury (then Lord Ashley) brought
in his Bills to do away with child
labour, not only in this way, but in
mines and factories.[1]   Also it sheds a
flood of light upon the condition of

[1] See Preface.

the little known world of the London sweeps.

The writer's assurance in pointing to himself as an example will not surprise those who knew his absolute simplicity and sincerity of character. The only thing necessary to say about it is that *it was true*, and that he could do it without giving offence.

His reference to his own life as that of a peacemaker calls up a vivid picture of a certain time where there was an "organ difficulty" at H——. Party feeling ran high, and no one was willing to preach on the week-night but Brother L——, who readily accepted the appointment. He gave out the characteristic text, "Behold, how good and pleasant a thing it is for brethren to dwell together in unity." The sermon was "straight from the shoulder," most timely, and withal so kindly that

every one loved him for his faithful
dealing, and went home resolved to do
better.

His resignation to the will of God, and
even triumph of joy, at the close of his
life, amid poverty and loss, the rapid
decline of his health, accompanied by a
racking cough, and other troubles of the
bitterest kind, are a most pathetic witness
to the consoling power of the religion of
Christ.

Our friend entered into the saints' ever-
lasting rest on 28th December 1896, at
the age (as this world counts age) of
sixty-four.

Shortly before his death he said to his
son, " I have nothing more to tell you,
only to live the same as I have lived."
He asked to have put on his tombstone
these words, and these only—

" JESUS—MY SAVIOUR."

To his youngest son, who was with him at the last, he said he was

> Sweeping through the gates of the new Jerusalem,
> Washed in the blood of the Lamb.

He also charged him to meet him in heaven.

The king of terrors had no power to terrify this bold servant of Christ. Almost his last conscious utterance was, " Jesus, mighty to save!" He was sitting up in bed when the end drew near. He remarked that it was getting rather dark, then sank into peaceful unconsciousness, and at length, without any pain or struggle, passed beyond the veil. The smile which now overspread his face seemed to tell that he had caught a vision of the King in His beauty, in that bright land where sorrow and pain cannot come.

Mr. T. C. Garland, for many years Seamen's Missionary at the port of London, writes : " I have known Mr. L—— for the last thirty-five years, and a more consistent Christian I never met. His conversion to God was real. His liberality in giving to the poor, his zeal in seeking out the sick and dying, in order to relieve their wants and tell them the 'story of the Cross,' were most remarkable. For power in prayer, and simple but mighty faith in pleading with God and with sinners, I have not known his equal.

" After his conversion he passed through great privations and persecutions, but he bore all in the spirit of meekness. On one occasion, between Amersham and Coleshill, he was assaulted and beaten by wicked men, who said '*they would drive his religion out of him.*' He often remarked afterwards in telling this incident, that 'they drove it more into him instead.'

"As he went through life he made many friends. Wherever he pitched his tent he built an altar, and he has left a name that will not soon be forgotten. I have met with many who have acknowledged him as their spiritual father, but not until the last great day will all the work of this true *man of God* be known."

NOTES

---◆---

NOTE A.

The reference to Feargus O'Connor on p. 26 recalls a curious experiment made by the Chartist leader of that name, who in the year 1839 purchased a farm at Heronsgate, described by an eye-witness as "one of the queerest villages on earth." He cut up the farm into allotments and built dwelling-houses for a number of weavers whom he imported from the north. The colony was called O'Connorville, a name by which some of the oldest inhabitants still know it. "Poverty and failure followed the scheme, but the allotments remain to this day, and in summer-time the scene is exceedingly beautiful — the orchards, gardens, and rustic houses presenting a unique picture." There is a small Wesleyan chapel at Heronsgate.

NOTE B.

Common Moor Mill is now known as Croxley Mill. It stands between Rickmansworth and Watford, and belongs to Messrs. Dickenson & Co. Here the paper for the *Strand Magazine* and *Black and White* is made. Loudwater Mill no longer exists.

PRINTED BY MORRISON AND GIBB LIMITED, EDINBURGH

www.ingramcontent.com/pod-product-compliance
Lightning Source LLC
Chambersburg PA
CBHW081517040426

42447CB00013B/3252